ENGLISH GRAMMAR AND EXERCISES
Book One

ENGLISH GRAMMAR AND EXERCISES

Book One

by L. R. H. CHAPMAN
illustrated by Daphne Rowles

LONGMAN

LONGMAN GROUP UK LIMITED
Longman House, Burnt Mill, Harlow,
Essex CM20 2JE, England
and Associated Companies throughout the world.

First published *1964
Fourty-eighth impression 1994

Printed in Malaysia by VVP

ISBN 0 – 582 – 52066 – 5

To the Teacher

This book, the first of a series, is intended for pupils who are in their *second* year of learning English as a foreign language, and who began English at approximately 10-11 years of age. Such pupils have already some acquaintance with the grammar of their mother-tongue and need, in the present writer's opinion, grammatical foundations to the English they learn to understand by ear and by eye, to speak, and to write in each year of study. It is believed that the laying of these foundations can and should begin in the second year of study.

The grammar in this book is functional, its aim being to develop pupils' ability to use English correctly, with some understanding, naturally limited by their small knowledge of the language, of the grammatical system at work. The grammatical forms and structures which are taught, and the vocabulary used in examples and exercises, apart perhaps from a few words (and these are common words), are all such as are normally met by pupils in their first year of English. The exercises have been framed so that average pupils *can* do them without entire dependence on the teacher. They should be done orally and/or in writing; many are arranged in sets, with the intention that one set can be done orally, and another in writing. Throughout the book, the attempt has been made to use in examples, and to produce from pupils in the exercises, English which is not only grammatically correct, but which also (within the limits imposed by elementary syntax and a small vocabulary) could be said and written naturally and in real situations by native English speakers.

Understanding of the examples, and ability to do the exercises with understanding of their meaning, will be the pupils' chief profit from this book. They must learn some grammatical terms, though these are used sparingly. They must also be given some grammatical explanations, but teachers should note that it is often impossible to express these in English which beginners can understand, and they will therefore find it necessary to render many of these explanations in the pupils' language. Similarly instructions on how to do exercises must sometimes be translated

The attention of teachers is called to one more point. The grammatical treatment is not exhaustive: there is, for example, much more to be learnt about 'uncountable' Nouns and the uses of 'shall' and 'will' than this book contains. But it seems wiser to reveal grammatical truth a little at a time, and it is proposed in subsequent books to expand the treatment of grammar begun here.

L.R.H.C.

Contents

1. The verbs *am, is, are*

Learn the Present Tense:

I am	We are
You are	You are
He is	
She is	They are
It is	

Put *am, is,* or *are* in the spaces:

1. The window ____ open.
2. Cats ____ small animals.
3. I ____ in the classroom.
4. We ____ pupils.
5. The baby ____ in bed.
6. You ____ a teacher.

1. The books ____ on the table.
2. I ____ a pupil.
3. My father ____ a good man.
4. We ____ in the classroom.
5. The door ____ shut.
6. The camel ____ a big animal.

1. The children ____ in the garden.
2. I ____ in school now.
3. The chair ____ behind the table.
4. Camels ____ big animals.
5. My mother ____ at home.
6. The windows ____ shut.

2. Nouns

What are nouns?

1. Nouns are words for persons, like these:
   boy, teacher, child, father, pupil, doctor.
2. Nouns are words for things and places, like these:
   book, chair, pen, school, cinema, garden.
3. Nouns are words for animals and other living things, like these:
   cat, camel, dog, fish, bird, tree.

Here are 18 nouns:

donkey, baby, policeman, car, house, hen, woman, pencil
mouse, animal, girl, field, flower, brother, window, city
soldier, horse.

Six of them are words for persons, six are words for things or places, and six are words for animals and other living things.
Put them under the right headings:

PERSONS   THINGS OR PLACES   ANIMALS AND OTHER
                                 LIVING THINGS

Here are 20 words. Only 12 of them are nouns. Find the nouns and write them.

mother, table, big, are, blackboard, man, two, door, box,
classroom, bed, the, tree, open, sister, desk, in, shut, bird,
behind.

3.   The verbs *am not, is not, are not*

Learn the Present Tense Negative. The Negative is made by adding *not*.

I am not	We are not
You are not	You are not
He is not	
She is not	They are not
It is not	

Put *am not, is not,* or *are not* in the spaces:

1. A thief __ ____ a good man.
2. Camels ____ ____ small animals.
3. I ____ ____ an old man (woman).
4. My hands ____ ____ dirty.
5. The poor man __ ____ happy.
6. We ____ ____ in the cinema now.

1. The mouse __ ____ a big animal.
2. I ____ ____ a teacher.
3. We ____ ____ at home now.
4. It __ ____ cold in summer.
5. My face __ ____ dirty.
6. The shops ____. ____ open every day.

Make true sentences:

I am I am not	a boy. a girl. a man. a woman. a pupil. a teacher.	We are We are not	boys. girls. men. women. pupils. teachers.

3

4. Plural Nouns (1)

The Plural of most Nouns is made by adding *s* to the Singular

SINGULAR	PLURAL
door	doors
cat	cats
boy	boys
bird	birds
book	books

The Plural of *a cat* is *cats*:

Singular: A cat is an animal.
Plural: Cats are animals.

Make these sentences Plural:

1. A pupil is not a teacher.
2. A hen is a bird.
3. He is a doctor.
4. She is a pretty girl.
5. Here is a pen and a pencil.
6. A camel is a big animal.
7. An egg is white.
8. There is a car behind you.
9. A donkey is bigger than a cat.
10. A lazy boy is not a good pupil.

The Plural of *the window* is *the windows:*

>*Singular:* The window is shut.
>*Plural:*   The windows are shut.

Make these sentences Plural:

1. The classroom is clean.
2. The teacher is not here every day.
3. The boy is in the garden.
4. The door is open.
5. The shop is shut today.
6. The book is on the desk.
7. Where is the key?
8. The pupil is not in the classroom.
9. The field is green.
10. The car is in the street.

Make these sentences Plural. Remember:

SINGULAR	PLURAL
a cat	cats
the window	the windows

1. There is a bird on the tree.
2. The soldier is on a horse.
3. There is a map on the wall of the classroom.
4. It is a picture of a flower.
5. The teacher of English is a good teacher.
6. The book is in a cupboard.
7. The lesson is an English lesson.
8. There is an egg in the basket.
9. The cow is in a field.
10. Where is the key of the door?

5. Questions with the verbs *am, is, are*

Learn the question form of the Present Tense. Questions are made by putting the verbs first:

Am I?	Are we?
Are you?	Are you?
Is he?	
Is she?	Are they?
Is it?	

Make questions from these mixed words:

Example: your hands / or dirty / are / clean
Question: Are your hands clean or dirty?

(Do not forget the capital letter and the question mark.)

1. near the school / your home / is
2. shut / the windows / are
3. your books / are / in your desk
4. is / in bed / the baby
5. or brown / your shoes / are / black
6. every day / is / this shop / open

1. camels / or small animals / are / big
2. in your bag / your ruler / is
3. open / this school / is / at night
4. all the pupils / here today / are
5. at home / your mother / is
6. good / are / or bad / those eggs

Many questions begin with *Is there a* or *Are there any*, for example:

Is there a cinema in this street?
Answers: Yes, there is. No, there is not.

Are there any pupils in the playground?
Answers: Yes, there are. No, there are not (none).

6

Make questions like these from these mixed words:

1. there / in the cupboard / are / any books
2. on the wall / is / a map / there
3. in this village / there / a school / is
4. are / in this book / any pictures / there
5. any flowers / there / are / in the garden
6. near this school / a river / there / is

1. are / on the tree / any apples / there
2. there / in this classroom / is / a cupboard
3. are / in the field / any horses / there
4. behind your house / there / a garden / is
5. any cars / are / in the street / there
6. a window / is / there / near the blackboard

There are many questions like this:

How many books are there on the table?

Short answer: There are six.
Long answer: There are six books on the table.

Make questions to which these are the long answers:

1. There are thirty pupils in this class.
2. There are three bedrooms in the house.
3. There are seven days in a week.
4. There are two schools in this village.
5. There are twenty pencils in the box.
6. There are twelve eggs in the basket.
7. There are four chairs in the room.
8. There are three rulers on the floor.
9. There are six words on the blackboard.
10. There are four maps on the wall.

6. Plural Nouns (2)

1. The Plural of some Nouns is made by adding *es* (pronounce *iz*) to the Singular.

   Learn:

SINGULAR	PLURAL
bus	buses
class	classes
glass	glasses
watch	watches
box	boxes

2. The Plural of Nouns like *baby* (ending in *y* with a consonant before it) is made by changing *y* into *ies*.

   Learn:

SINGULAR	PLURAL
baby	babies
city	cities
lady	ladies

3. Some Nouns have different Singular and Plural forms.

   Learn:

SINGULAR	PLURAL
man	men
woman	women
child	children
foot	feet
tooth	teeth
knife	knives
thief	thieves
mouse	mice .

…ay and write how many there are in the pictures. The first one … done for you.

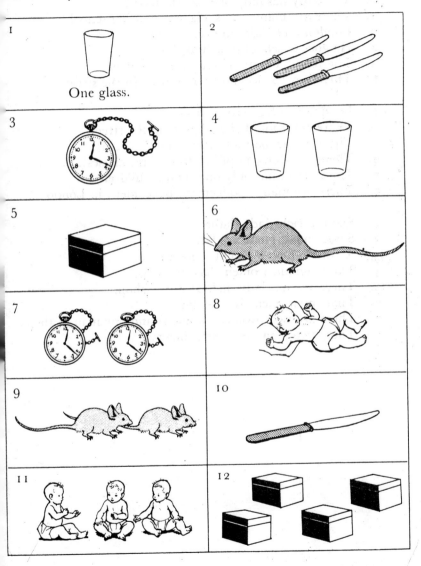

1 One glass.	2
3	4
5	6
7	8
9	10
11	12

Choose the right word:

1. The baby has only one (tooth, teeth).
2. There are many (class, classes) in a big school.
3. London and Cairo are (city, cities).
4. He goes to school in a (bus, buses).
5. The (child, children) are in the garden.
6. There is a (policeman, policemen) in the street.

1. London is a big (city, cities).
2. There are a lot of (bus, buses) in the street.
3. The old man has only three (tooth, teeth).
4. There are thirty pupils in this (class, classes).
5. The woman has only one (child, children).
6. There are many (policeman, policemen) in London.

1. She is a rich (lady, ladies).
2. Some (man, men) are fat.
3. A (thief, thieves) is not a good man.
4. The (woman, women) has two sons.
5. There are six (lady, ladies) in the shop.
6. That (man, men) is a doctor.
7. There are two (woman, women) and one man in the car.
8. Those two men are (thief, thieves).

7. The Present Continuous Tense (1)

Look at this picture and sentence:

The teacher is standing near the blackboard NOW, while the pupil is saying the sentence. The teacher continues to stand near the blackboard while the pupil is speaking.

We call *is standing* the Present Continuous Tense. It is made with:

is + stand + ing

Verbs have stems, like flowers. *stand* is the stem of the verb, we add *ing* to it, and make *standing*.

Learn the Present Continuous Tense of *stand*:

	NEGATIVE	QUESTION
I am standing.	I am not standing.	Am I standing?
You are standing.	You are not standing.	Are you standing?
He is standing.	He is not standing.	Is he standing?
She is standing.	She is not standing.	Is she standing?
It is standing.	It is not standing.	Is it standing?
We are standing.	We are not standing.	Are we standing?
You are standing.	You are not standing.	Are you standing?
They are standing.	They are not standing.	Are they standing?

Oral Exercise

Practise saying the Present Continuous Tense (with Negative and Question forms) of these verb stems:

go drink eat jump play walk climb fall

Answer (orally and/or in writing) the questions about the pictures. Use the verb stems in brackets.

1. What is the girl doing?
   She __ _____ a book. (read)

2. What are the boys doing?
   They ____ _____ football. (play)

3. What is the teacher doing?
   He __ _____ the blackboard. (clean)

4. What are the cats doing?
   They ____ _____ the tree. (climb)

5. What is the man doing?
   He __ _____ an apple. (eat)

6. What are the children doing?
   They ____ _____ across the road. (walk)

Put the Present Continuous Tense in the spaces in each sentence.
Use the verb stems in brackets. (The teacher should first check
the pupils' understanding of these verb stems, if necessary.)

1. The horse __ _____ over the wall. (jump)
2. I ____ _____ English now. (learn)
3. The woman __ _____ her baby. (carry)
4. The boys ____ _____ to school. (go)
5. The old man __ _____ a cup of tea. (drink)
6. Two policemen ____ _____ outside the bank.
   (stand)

1. The servant __ _____ the floor. (wash)
2. The men ____ _____ a house. (build)
3. The plane __ _____ to London. (fly)
4. The children ____ _____ in the garden. (play)
5. The thief __ _____ the window. (open)
6. The teacher __ _____ English. (teach)

8. The Present Continuous Tense (2)

If the verb stem ends with the letter *e*, the Present Continuous Tense is made like this:

STEM	PRESENT CONTINUOUS TENSE
come	I am coming, etc. NO *e*
drive	I am driving, etc.
give	I am giving, etc.
live	I am living, etc.
make	I am making, etc.
ride	I am riding, etc.
write	I am writing, etc.

Write these sentences, putting Present Continuous Tenses in the spaces. Use the verb stems in brackets.

1. The boy __ _____ a bicycle. (ride)
2. The soldiers ____ _____ in tents. (live)
3. I ____ _____ a letter. (write)
4. The doctor __ _____ a car. (drive)
5. The children ____ _____ home from school. (come)
6. The teacher __ _____ an English lesson. (give)
7. The carpenter __ _____ a table. (make)

If a short verb stem ends with the letter *g*, *m*, *n*, or *t* (with a short vowel sound before it), the Present Continuous Tense is made like this:

14

STEM	PRESENT CONTINUOUS TENSE	
dig	I am digging, etc.	*gg*
swim	I am swimming, etc.	*mm*
run	I am running, etc.	*nn*
cut	I am cutting, etc.	*tt*
get	I am getting, etc.	*tt*
put	I am putting, etc.	*tt*
shut	I am shutting, etc.	*tt*
sit	I am sitting, etc.	*tt*

Write these sentences, putting Present Continuous Tenses in the spaces. Use the verb stems in brackets.

1. We ____ _____ in the classroom. (sit)
2. I ____ _____ the books into the cupboard. (put)
3. The woman __ _____ the bread with a knife. (cut)
4. The boys ___ _____ in the river. (swim)
5. The old man __ _____ out of the bus. (get)
6. The little girl __ _____ to school. (run)
7. The servants ___ _____ the windows. (shut)

9. Proper Nouns

Names of real persons and places are called Proper Nouns. The MUST begin with a capital letter:

Names of real persons:

Boys or men: Jack, Ahmad, Bob, Yusef, Tom, Ali.
Girls or women: Mary, Hala, Jane, Fatma, Ann, Abla.

Names of real places:

Countries: England, Egypt, India, China, France, America
Cities: London, Cairo, Paris, New York, Beirut, Tokyo

The days of the week, and the months of the year, are Prope Nouns, and MUST begin with a capital letter:

Sunday, Monday, Tuesday, Wednesday, Thursday, Friday Saturday.

January, February, March, April, May, June, July, August September, October, November, December.

Read these sentences, and notice the Proper Nouns, which begin with a capital letter:

1. The Queen of England has a palace in London.
2. The River Nile is in Africa.
3. The name Ahmad is the name of an Arab.
4. There are many Englishmen in India.
5. It is very cold in Russia in December and January.
6. The capital of France is Paris.

Write these sentences again, using capital letters for the Proper Nouns. The number of Proper Nouns in each sentence is put in brackets.

1. My friend ali is going to france in april. (3)
2. The shops in london are shut on sunday. (2)
3. It is very hot in cairo in july and august. (3)
4. The plane is flying from beirut to paris. (2)
5. My friend jack is an englishman. (2)
6. Her sister mary is living in america. (2)

10. Adjectives

Adjectives are words which tell us something about Nouns. Look at the sentence under the picture:

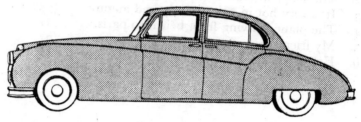

This is a *big* car.

big is an Adjective. It tells us something about the Noun *car*.

We can write this sentence in another way:

This car is *big*.

Learn these Adjectives:

fat   thin   rich   poor   young   old   tall   short

Say or write 2 sentences like these about each picture:

1. This is a fat man.
2. This man is fat.

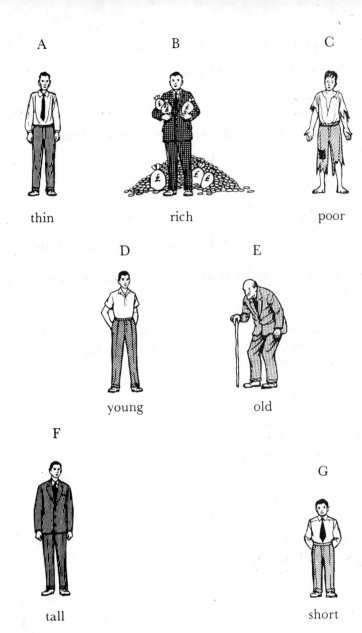

A

thin

B

rich

C

poor

D

young

E

old

F

tall

G

short

In Lesson 4 we learnt:

SINGULAR	PLURAL
a cat	cats
the window	the windows

We follow the same way if there is an Adjective before the Noun:

SINGULAR	PLURAL
a fat boy	fat boys
the fat boy	the fat boys

Learn these Adjectives:

good   bad   clean   dirty   black   red   gold   little   pretty

Copy these words, and put them in the Plural. Numbers 1 and 2 are done for you.

	SINGULAR	PLURAL
1.	a bad tooth	bad teeth
2.	the gold watch	the gold watches
3.	a good teacher	
4.	the clean glass	
5.	a black cat	
6.	a dirty foot	
7.	the red pencil	
8.	a little child	
9.	the pretty flower	

11. The Present Continuous Tense (3)

Negative Sentences and Questions

Look at these 2 sentences:

       The girl is standing on a chair.
       She is not standing on a table.

Complete the following sentences in the same way:

1.

The pupil __ _____ the blackboard.
He __ not cleaning the floor.

2.

The two boys ____ riding bicycles.
They are ____ _____ horses.

3.

The man __ _____ his face.
He __ ____ washing his feet.

4.

The woman __ walking up the hill.
She __ ____ _____ down the hill.

5.

The pupils ____ _____ in the classroom.
They ____ ____ sitting in the cinema.

6.

The woman __ opening the window.
She __ __ __ the door.

7.

The man __ __ a car.
He __ __ driving a bus.

8.

The children __ going home.
They __ __ __ to school.

9.

The horse __ jumping over a gate.
It __ __ __ over a wall.

10.

The boy __ __ an apple.
He __ __ eating an egg.

Look at this question and answer:

Where is the boy swimming?
In the river.

omplete the following questions. Begin each with *Where.* Here
re the 5 verb stems which you must use:

write go stand put sit

1.
_____ __ the baby _____ ?
On the floor.

2.
_____ are the boys _____ ?
To school.

3.
_____ __ the teacher _____ the books?
In the cupboard.

4.
_____ __ the pupil _____ ?
On the blackboard.

5.
_____ ____ the two girls _____ ?
Under the tree.

Look at this question and answer:

What is the boy eating?
An apple.

23

Complete the following questions. Begin each with *What*. Her are the 5 verb stems which you must use:

ride   build   wash   clean   drink

1.

———— — the man ———— ?

His shoes.

2.

———— are the soldiers ————

Horses.

3.

———— — the cat ———— ?

Milk.

4.

———— — the girl ————

Her hands.

5.

———— —— the men ———— ?

A wall.

12. Subject Pronouns

Pronouns are words which we use instead of Nouns. Look at these pairs of sentences:

The teacher is in the classroom.
He is writing on the blackboard.

He in the second sentence is a Pronoun. It is used instead of the Noun *teacher*. It is better to say or write *He* than to say or write again *The teacher*.

The woman is in a shop. *She* is carrying a bag.

She in the second sentence is a Pronoun. It is used instead of the Noun *woman*.

The book is on the table. *It* is an English book.

It in the second sentence is a Pronoun. It is used instead of the Noun *book*.

The cat is in the kitchen. *It* is drinking milk.

It in the second sentence is a Pronoun. It is used instead of the Noun *cat*. So we see that the Pronoun *it* can be used for things like *book* or animals like *cat*.

The boys are in the playground.
They are playing football.

The women are in the shop.
They are buying shoes.

The mice are in the kitchen.
They are eating the bread.

The books are in the cupboard.
They are English books.

They is a Pronoun. It is used instead of *boys* (or *men*), *women* (or *girls*), animals like *mice*, and things like *books*.

Now look at these pairs of sentences:

1. *The man* is kicking the donkey. *He* is a bad man.
2. *The donkey* is kicking the man. *It* is a bad donkey.

In the first pair of sentences, *The man* is the Subject. He is doing something. He is kicking the donkey. So *He* is a Subject Pronoun.

In the second pair of sentences, *The donkey* is the Subject. It is doing something. It is kicking the man. So *It* is a Subject Pronoun.

The Subject Pronouns are:

SINGULAR	PLURAL
I	We
You	You
He	They
She	They
It	They

Put Subject Pronouns in the spaces in the second of each pair of sentences:

1. The window is open. ___ is not shut.
2. The policeman is standing in the street. ___ is a tall man.
3. The pencils are in the box. _____ are red pencils.
4. The girl is at home. _____ is cooking.
5. The plane is in the air. ___ is flying to London.
6. The birds are on the tree. _____ are singing.
7. The doctor is a rich man. ___ is driving a big car.
8. The teacher is a woman. _____ is teaching the little children.

1. The children are in the garden. _____ are playing.
2. The woman is poor. _____ is living in a little house.
3. The horse is in the field. ___ is eating the grass.
4. The shops are shut today. _____ are not open.
5. The fisherman is catching fish. ___ is in a boat.
6. The girl is in bed. _____ is sleeping.
7. The key is not in the desk. ___ is in the box.
8. I am sitting beside (Name). ___ are friends.

13. The verbs *have, has*

Learn the Present Tense:

SINGULAR	PLURAL
I have	We have
You have	You have
He has	
She has	They have
It has	

Put *have* or *has* in *the spaces:*

1. A camel _____ four legs.
2. I _____ ten fingers.
3. The baby _____ two teeth.
4. The old man _____ white hair.
5. Donkeys _____ big ears.
6. The poor woman _____ five children.
7. Some dogs _____ long tails.
8. Mr. and Mrs. Brown _____ one son.

have got and *has got* have the same meaning as *have* and *has*. If you put *have* or *has* correctly in the spaces above, the sentences will be good English. They would also be right if you put *have got* or *has got*.

Note to the teacher: There is a difference between the first and second set of 8 sentences. In the first set, the Object in each sentence is a part of the Subject: *four legs* are a part of *a camel*; *white hair* is a part of *the old man*, etc. In the second set, the Object in each sentence is a thing or things belonging to the Subject: *the pencils* belong to *the pupils*; *the car* belongs to *the doctor*, etc. It is not possible to make a rule, but it seems more usual to say *have got* or *has got* when one is speaking of belongings which are not a physical part or parts of the possessor(s).

Put *have got* or *has got* in the spaces:

1. All the pupils _____ _____ pencils.
2. The doctor _____ _____ a new car.
3. My father _____ _____ a gold watch.
4. Ali and his brother _____ _____ new shoes.
5. I _____ _____ a pen and a pencil in my pocket.
6. We _____ _____ some pretty flowers in the garden.
7. The rich woman _____ _____ a lot of dresses.
8. My brother _____ _____ a bicycle.

14. *have got, has got*

Questions

In questions, *have got* and *has got* are much more common than *have* and *has* only, so we will learn and use these question forms:

SINGULAR | PLURAL
Have I got? | Have we got?
Have you got? | Have you got?
Has he got? |
Has she got? | Have they got?
Has it got? |

Look at these questions and the short answers to them. Notice that *got* is not used in the answers.

Have you got a clean handkerchief? Yes, I have.

Has the teacher got a car? No, he has not.

Make questions from these mixed words. Do not forget the capital letter and the question mark.

1. rulers / got / all the pupils / have
2. the girl / has / a new dress / got
3. got / in your pocket / have / any money / you
4. has / the key / got / the teacher
5. a bicycle / got / has / the policeman
6. on their heads / have / got / the children / hats
7. got / your brother / has / a watch
8. have / guns / the soldiers / got

Look at the picture, and read the question and answer about it.

What has the teacher got in his hand?
A stick.

Make questions about the pictures from these mixed words. The answers are given.

I.

the cat / got / what / in its mouth / has
A mouse.

2.

has / on her fingers / the woman / what / got
Rings.

3.

got / the boy / what / has / in his hand
A bird.

4.

on their heads / what / got / have / the women
Water pots.

5.

what / these two girls / have / got
New watches.

6.

has / what / on its back / got / the donkey
A big bag.

15. *have got, has got*

Negative Sentences

Learn these Negative forms, which are very commonly used:

SINGULAR	PLURAL
I haven't got	We haven't got
You haven't got	You haven't got
He hasn't got	
She hasn't got	They haven't got
It hasn't got	

Learn how *haven't* and *hasn't* are made and written:

have or *has* and *not* are joined, and the letter *o* of *not* is left out. The apostrophe is put in the place of the letter *o*.

Put *haven't got* or *hasn't got* in the spaces:

1. The poor boy _____ ____ a bicycle.
2. We _____ ____ a holiday today.
3. The little girl _____ ____ a watch.
4. I _____ ____ the key of the door.
5. Ahmad _____ ____ any ink in his pen.
6. The poor children _____ ____ shoes.

1. The baby _____ ____ much hair.
2. I _____ ____ many flowers in my garden.
3. The fishermen _____ ____ big nets.
4. Jack _____ ____ a lot of money.
5. A small school _____ ____ a big playground.
6. The pupils _____ ____ any paper.

16. Object Pronouns

In Lesson 12 we learnt and used Subject Pronouns. Look again at this sentence:

The man is kicking the donkey.

The man is the Subject of the sentence, because he is doing the action. So, instead of *The man*, we can use the Subject Pronoun *He*, and say:

He is kicking the donkey.

the donkey is the Object of the sentence. The donkey is not doing anything. So, instead of *the donkey*, we can use the Object Pronoun *it*, and say:

He is kicking it.

Look again at this sentence from Lesson 12:

The donkey is kicking the man.

In this sentence, *The donkey* is the Subject, so we can use the Subject Pronoun *it* (the Object Pronoun is the same). *the man* is the Object. He is not doing anything. So, instead of *the man*, we can use the Object Pronoun *him*, and make the sentence:

It is kicking him.

Here are the Subject and Object Pronouns:

SINGULAR		PLURAL	
Subject	*Object*	*Subject*	*Object*
I	me	we	us
you	you	you	you
he	him		
she	her	they	them
it	it		

33

write the following sentences again, using Object instead of the words in italics.

1. The policeman is running after *the thief*.
2. The teacher is cleaning *the blackboard*.
3. The boys are riding *bicycles*.
4. The doctor is looking at *the girl*.
5. Please open *the windows*.
6. The woman is carrying *a bag*.
7. The servant is washing *the little girl*.
8. The children are standing near *the old man*.

B. Put Object Pronouns in the spaces:

1. The soldiers are riding horses. They are riding _____ up the hill.
2. We are learning English. The teacher is teaching __ English.
3. The teacher has got a lot of books. He is putting _____ in the cupboard.
4. The little girl is drinking milk. She is drinking __ from a glass.
5. He is sitting beside the girl, and looking at _____ .
6. The woman is taking the little boy to the hospital. She is carrying _____ in her arms.
7. I am a pupil, and the teacher is teaching __ English.
8. The servant is washing the floor. She is washing __ with soap and water.

C. Put the right Subject Pronoun in the first space, and the right Object Pronoun in the second space:

1. The boy is writing on the blackboard.
   __ is writing on __ with chalk.
2. The woman is opening the windows.
   _____ is not shutting _____ .
3. Jack is sitting in front of Mary.
   __ is not sitting behind _____ .

34

4. The men are building a wall.

       _____ are building ___ with bricks.

5. The doctor has got a boy in his car.

       __ is taking _____ to the hospital.

6. The children are eating apples.

       _____ are eating _____ in the garder

17. Nouns without Plurals

When we say *a cat* or *an egg*, we mean one cat or one egg. We can say three cats, five eggs, etc., because we can count cats or eggs.

But we CANNOT say *a milk*, because this would mean *one milk*. What is *one milk?* What are *two milks?* These questions have no sense and cannot be answered, because we cannot count milk.

We can use the Noun *milk* in these ways:

The milk is in the jug.
The cat is drinking *milk*.
The girl is drinking *a glass of milk*.
There is *a drop of milk* on the table.
There are *two bottles of milk* in the kitchen.

We learn from these sentences that:

We can use the Noun *milk* with *the*.
We can use it without *the*.
We can NEVER use it with *a*.
We can NEVER say *milks*.

We cannot count *milk*, but we can count:
drops of milk, glasses of milk, bottles of milk, jugs of milk, etc.

Here are 9 other Nouns like *milk*:

ink, coffee, tea, water, bread, chalk, paper, soap, money.

Put one of these 9 Nouns into each space:

1. The poor man has got no _____ in his pocket.
2. The teacher is writing on the blackboard with _____ .
3. The servant is washing the floor with _____ and _____ .

4. Jack is drinking _____ , but Mary is drinking ____
5. The children are eating _____ and butter.
6. The ____ in this bottle is red.
7. The pupils are writing on _____

Here are some ways of using Nouns without Plurals:

a piece of soap   pieces of chalk
a piece of paper   cups of coffee
a glass of water   bottles of ink
a lot of money

Use these 7 ways to complete the following sentences:

1. There are only three _____ — _____ in the chalk box.
2. The rich man has got __ ____ __ _____ .
3. The men are drinking ___ __ _____ , but the little boy is drinking __ _____ __ _____ .
4. The pupil is writing on __ _____ __ _____ .
5. There are twenty _____ — ____ in the cup-board in the classroom.
6. She is washing her hands with __ _____ __ ___

Nouns without Plurals are often used with the word *no* in front of them. In the first exercise in this lesson, we had the sentence:

The poor man has got *no money* in his pocket.

Here is another sentence of the same kind:

There is *no milk* in the kitchen.

Complete these sentences, using in each *no* and one of these
7 Nouns:

bread, chalk, ink, paper, soap, tea, water.

1. The pupils have __ _____ to write on.
2. There is __ _____ in this little river in the summer.
3. I have got __ ____ in my pen.
4. There is __ _____ in the chalk box.
5. The poor children have __ _____ to eat.
6. There is __ _____ in the bathroom.
7. We are drinking coffee, because we have __ ____

18. The Present Tense (1)

In Lesson 7, we learnt that verbs have stems. We use the stem of the verb to make the Present Tense:

Stem—drink

PRESENT TENSE

SINGULAR	PLURAL
I drink	We drink
You drink	You drink
He drinks·	
She drinks	They drink
It drinks	

s is added to the stem after the Pronouns *he*, *she*, and *it*, or after Nouns for which these Pronouns are used:

He drinks
The man drinks
The boy drinks

She drinks
The girl drinks
The woman drinks

It drinks
The cat drinks

Practise saying (fairly quickly) the Present Tense of these verb stems, or of some of them:

stand, sit, eat, play, jump, walk, run, climb, come, live, swim.

We can learn the meaning of the Present Tense, and when to use it, from these sentences:

1. Jack walks to school every morning.
2. The teacher rides to school on a bicycle.

3. We learn English at school.
4. Doctors work hard.
5. Donkeys eat grass.
6. I go to bed at ten o'clock.
7. The boys play football every afternoon.
8. My mother cooks every day.

These sentences show that we must use the Present Tense to describe actions which happen regularly, every morning, every afternoon, every day, etc. For example:

Jack walks to school *every morning*.

And the second sentence means that the teacher regularly rides to school on a bicycle.

We must also use the Present Tense to describe actions which are always or generally true. For example:

Doctors work hard.

Choose the right verb in each sentence from the two verbs in brackets:

1. Mary (run, runs) to school every morning.
2. We (speak, speaks) English in the English lesson.
3. The rich man (live, lives) in a big house.
4. I (drink, drinks) a glass of milk every morning.
5. My father (read, reads) the newspaper every day.
6. My father (give, gives) me pocket-money every week.
7. Cats (eat, eats) mice.
8. A teacher (work, works) hard.
9 I (clean, cleans) my teeth three times a day.
10. The shopkeeper (open, opens) his shop at nine o'clock.

Look at this sentence:

I *like* apples, but my brother *likes* oranges.

Complete the following sentences in the same way. Use one of these verb stems in each sentence:

walk, come, write, live, drink, play.

1. I _____ with a pen, but my little brother _____ with a pencil.
2. I _____ tea, but my little brother _____ milk.
3. I _____ on two legs, but a horse _____ on four legs.
4. I _____ in a house, but a king _____ in a palace.
5. I _____ with a ball, but my sister _____ with a doll.
6. I _____ to school early, but Tom always _____ late.

Learn this:

es is added to some verb stems after the Pronouns *he*, *she*, and *it*, or after Nouns for which these Pronouns are used.

VERB STEMS

go	*do*	*wash*	*catch*	*teach*
He goes	He does	He washes	He catches	He teaches
She goes	She does	She washes	She catches	She teaches
It goes	It does	It washes	It catches	It teaches

Learn this also:

When a verb stem ends with the letter *y*, with a consonant before it, the Present Tense after the Pronouns *he*, *she*, and *it*, or after Nouns for which these Pronouns are used, is made like this:

Verb stem *fly*	Verb stem *carry*
He flies	He carries
She flies	She carries
It flies	It carries

19. The Present Tense (2)

Negative Sentences

Here is the Negative of the Present Tense of the verb stem *drink*:

SINGULAR

I do not drink
You do not drink
He does not drink
She does not drink
It does not drink

PLURAL

We do not drink
You do not drink

They do not drink

The Negative is made in this way:

do or *does* + *not* + verb stem *drink*

Practise saying (fairly quickly) the Present Tense Negative of these, or of some of these verb stems:

stand, sit, eat, jump, walk, run, climb, go, swim, come, carry.

Look at these sentences:

The little girl *drinks* milk. She *does not drink* coffee.
I *live* in a house. I *do not live* in a palace.

Fill in the spaces, and make sentences like those above:

1. We sleep at night. We __ ___ ___ in the daytime.
2. The soldier rides a horse. He ___ ___ ___ a donkey.
3. The boy ___ in the garden. He ___ ___ play in school.
4. Fishermen catch fish. They __ ___ ___ animals.

5. Mary _____ to school every day. She ___ ___ go to the cinema every day.

6. We speak English in the English lesson. We __ ___ _____ English at home.

1. Mr. Brown _____ English. He ___ ___ teach French.

2. A good pupil works hard. A lazy pupil ___ ___ _____ hard.

3. I see my father every day. I __ ___ ___ the doctor every day.

4. The doctor _____ a car. He ___ ___ drive a bus.

5. We learn English at school. We ___ ___ _____ French.

6. Cats eat mice. They __ ___ ___ dogs.

20. Possessive Forms

Look at this sentence:

The doctor has a new car.

The sentence means that the doctor *possesses* a new car, that the car *belongs* to him. We can also say:

The doctor's car is new.

doctor's is the Possessive form of the Singular Noun *doctor*. We make the Possessive form by adding *'s* (apostrophe *s*) to the Singular Noun. We use this Possessive form for persons and sometimes for animals. Here are some examples:

The boy's bicycle   The dog's tail
The teacher's book   The lion's teeth
My father's shoes   The cat's eyes

Look at these two sentences:

The boy has a dirty face.
The boy's face is dirty.

Complete the following sentences in the same way by using the Possessive form of the Noun. The first sentence is done for you.

1. The girl has a pretty dress.
   The girl's dress is pretty.
2. The old man has white hair.
   ____ ____ _____ _____ is white.
3. Mary has red shoes.
   _____ _____ are red.
4. The king has a beautiful palace.
   ____ _____ _____ is beautiful.
5. Ali has a new bicycle.
   _____ _____ is new.

6. The cat has green eyes.

___ ____ _____ are green.

7. My dog has a long tail.

___ ____ _____ is long.

8. The lion has sharp teeth.

___ .____ _____ are sharp.

Now look at these two sentences:

The pupils have clean hands.
The pupils' hands are clean.

pupils' is the Possessive form of the Plural Noun *pupils*. We make it by adding an apostrophe to the Plural Noun. So the Singular and Plural Possessive forms are:

SINGULAR	PLURAL
pupil's	pupils'
boy's	boys'
teacher's	teachers'
cat's	cats'
lion's	lions'

Complete the second sentence in each of the following pairs of sentences by using the Possessive form of the Plural Noun as in the second sentence above:

1. All the girls have new dresses.

All ___ ____ _____ are new.

2. The teachers have a room near the playground.

___ ____ _____ is near the playground.

3. All the soldiers have white horses.

All ___ ____ _____ are white.

4. The pupils have rulers on their desks.

___ ____ _____ are on their desks.

5. The servants have a bedroom near the kitchen.

___ ____ _____ is near the kitchen.

6. Donkeys have long ears.

____ _____ are long.

45

7. Some boys have blue eyes.
   Some _____ _____ are blue.
8. Some dogs have short tails.
   Some _____ _____ are short.

In Lesson 6 we learnt that some Nouns have different Singular and Plural forms. We make the Possessive form of these Nouns by adding 's (apostrophe s) to the Singular AND to the Plural Noun.

SINGULAR	PLURAL
man's	men's
woman's	women's
child's	children's
policeman's	policemen's
fisherman's	fishermen's

Complete the second sentence in each of the following pairs of sentences by using the Possessive form of the Singular or of the Plural Noun:

1. Those children have dirty faces.
   Those _____ _____ are dirty.
2. The woman has a very tall son.
   ___ _____ ___ is very tall.
3. The fishermen have an old net.
   ___ _____ ___ is old.
4. The child has a new toy.
   ___ _____ ___ is new.
5. That man has a very big nose.
   That _____ _____ is very big.
6. Some women have short hair.
   Some _____ _____ is short.
7. All the men have black hats.
   All ___ _____ _____ are black.

46

21. The Present Tense (3)

Questions

These are the question forms of the Present Tense of the verb
stem *drink*:

SINGULAR	PLURAL
Do I drink?	Do we drink?
Do you drink?	Do you drink?
Does he drink?	
Does she drink?	Do they drink?
Does it drink?	

Present Tense questions are made in this way:

do or *does* + Subject (Noun or Pronoun) + verb stem

Notice that the verb stem (and also in Negative sentences) does
NOT change. It is always *drink*.

Practise saying (fairly quickly) the Present Tense question forms
of these, or of some of these verb stems:

go, come, walk, run, climb, carry, see, work, sleep, live.

Put *Do* or *Does* in the spaces:

1. ———— you live in a palace?
2. ———— your father give you pocket-money?
3. ———— you clean your teeth every morning?
4. ———— pupils take their books home?
5. ———— a dog drink coffee?
6. ———— policemen work at night?
7. ———— Jack come to school early or late?
8. ———— the servant wash the floor every day?

47

1. _____ you like oranges or apples?
2. _____ your mother cook every day?
3. _____ I teach you English or French?
4. _____ you see your father every day?
5. _____ babies eat a lot of meat?
6. _____ Mary go to the cinema every week?
7. _____ the doctor drive a car?
8. _____ boys or girls play football?

Make questions from these mixed words:

Example: coffee / do you / in the morning / drink / or tea
Question: Do you drink coffee or tea in the morning?

(Do not forget the capital letter and the question mark.)

1. work hard / lazy men / do
2. on a bicycle / does / to school / come / the teacher
3. after school / you / do / go home
4. English / speak / your father / does
5. go to bed / little children / do / early or late
6. does / in a little house / live / the king
7. you / in a bus / go / do / to school
8. his teeth / Jack / every day / clean / does

Look at this question and the answers to it:

Where does the Queen of England live?
Short answer: In London.
Full answer: She lives in London.

Complete the following questions. Begin each with *Where*. The full answers are given.

1. _____ _____ your friend _____ ?
   He sits at the back of the class.
2. _____ _ you _____ English?
   We learn English at school.

48

3. _____ _____ the rich man ____ his money?
   He puts it in a bank.
4. _____ __ pupils _____ ?
   They play in the playground.
5. _____ _____ the doctor _____ ?
   He works in the hospital.
6. _____ __ fishermen _____ fish?
   They catch fish in the sea.

Look at this question and the answers to it:

When do you wash your hands and face?
Short answer: In the morning.
Full answer: I wash them in the morning.

Complete the following questions. Begin each with *When*. The full answers are given.

1. _____ _____ your father ____ __ ?
   He gets up at six o'clock.
2. _____ __ you __ __ ____ ?
   I go to bed at ten o'clock.
3. _____ _____ your father _____ _____ ?
   He comes home in the evening.
4. _____ __ you ____ __ your clothes?
   I put them on in the morning.
5. _____ _____ the first lesson _____ ?
   It begins at eight o'clock.
6. _____ __ the boys _____ _____ ?
   They play football on Saturday afternoon.

49

22. Possessive Forms of Pronouns

We learnt in Lesson 20 the Possessive forms of Nouns. Pronouns have Possessive forms also. The following sentences are written in two ways, (a) with the Possessive form of the Noun, and (b) with the Possessive form of the Pronoun used instead of the Noun.

1. (a) *The man's* hair is white.
   (b) *His* hair is white.
2. (a) *The girl's* dress is pretty.
   (b) *Her* dress is pretty.
3. (a) *The cat's* eyes are green.
   (b) *Its* eyes are green.
4. (a) *The men's* shoes are dirty.
   (b) *Their* shoes are dirty.
5. (a) *The women's* dresses are new.
   (b) *Their* dresses are new.
6. (a) *Donkeys'* ears are long.
   (b) *Their* ears are long.

From these sentences we can learn the Possessive forms of the Subject Pronouns (see Lesson 12) *he, she, it,* and *they.* We learnt the Object Pronouns in Lesson 16, so we can now make a list of the 3 forms of the Pronouns we have learnt:

SINGULAR			PLURAL		
Subject	*Object*	*Possessive*	*Subject*	*Object*	*Possessive*
I	me	my	we	us	our
you	you	your	you	you	your
he	him	his			
she	her	her	they	them	their
it	it	its			

Notice that the Plural form of *he, she,* and *it* is *they;* that the Plural form of *him, her,* and *it* is *them;* and that the Plural form of *his, her,* and *its* is *their.*

Put *his*, *her*, *its*, or *their* in place of the Nouns in the Possessive form (in italics):

1. *The king's* palace is very beautiful.
2. *The lion's* teeth are sharp.
3. *Jack's* little brother does not go to school.
4. *The girl's* mother is cooking in the kitchen.
5. *The pupils'* books are on the desks.
6. The child is pulling *the cat's* tail.
7. *Mary's* father is a doctor.
8. The teachers are sitting in *the teachers'* room.

1. The servant is washing *the girl's* dress.
2. Where is *the bird's* nest?
3. *The children's* hands and faces are clean.
4. *Ahmad's* father is a teacher.
5. Where does *Mary's* sister live?
6. *Women's* hair is long.
7. There are two boys on *the donkey's* back.
8. The policeman is holding *the thief's* arm.

Put the right forms of Pronouns in the spaces:

1. I love ___ mother, and my mother loves ___ .
2. Do you love _____ mother? Does your mother love ____ ?
3. Jack loves ____ mother, and his mother loves ____ .
4. Mary loves her mother, and ____ mother loves ____ .
5. Does a kitten love ____ mother? Does its mother love ___ ?
6. We all love ____ mothers, and our mothers love ___ .
7. Children love _____ mothers, and their mothers love _____ .
8. Cats wash their kittens. They wash _____ with _____ tongues.

23. Comparative Adjectives

Look at these sentences:

> Jack is twelve years old.
> Mary is ten years old.
> Jack is *older than* Mary.
> Mary is *younger than* Jack.

old and *young* are Adjectives (see Lesson 10). We are comparing the ages of Jack and Mary, so we must use Comparative Adjectives. These are made by adding *er* to the Adjective. After Comparative Adjectives we often need to use the word *than*.

Here are 4 Adjectives and their Comparative forms:

rich	richer
poor	poorer
tall	taller
short	shorter

Put one of these Comparative Adjectives followed by *than* in each space:

1. A servant is _____ _____ a king.
2. A king is _____ _____ a servant.
3. A boy is _____ _____ a man.
4. A man is _____ _____ a boy.

Notice the spelling of these Adjectives and their Comparative forms:

fat	fatter	(tt)	happy	happier	(ier)
hot	hotter	(tt)	dirty	dirtier	(ier)
big	bigger	(gg)	pretty	prettier	(ier)
thin	thinner	(nn)	hungry	hungrier	(ier)

Look at the pictures, and complete the following sentences by using the Comparative forms of these Adjectives: big, clean, dirty, fat, small, thin. Put *than* in the second space in each sentence.

1. Jack is _____ _____ Tom.
2. Tom is _____ _____ Jack.

 Jack    Tom

1. The girl's face is _____ _____ the boy's face.
2. The boy's face is _____ _____ the girl's face.

1. The box A is _____ _____ the box B.
2. The box B is _____ _____ the box A.

 A   B

Complete the following sentences by using the Comparative form of these Adjectives: cold, hot, hungry, pretty. Put *than* in the second space in each sentence.

1. Summer is _____ _____ winter.
2. Mary is _____ _____ her sister.
3. Poor men are often _____ _____ rich men.
4. Winter is _____ _____ summer.

There are a few Adjectives which have different words for their Comparative forms. Here are 2 which you must know:

good   better
bad   worse

Read these sentences and complete the two last by using the Comparative form of *good* or *bad*:

Jack's mark for handwriting is 8 out of 10.
Tom's mark for handwriting is 4 out of 10.
Jack's mark is _____ _____ Tom's mark.
Tom's mark is _____ _____ Jack's mark.

24. The Present Tense and the Present Continuous Tense

We learnt in Lesson 18 that the Present Tense is used to describe actions which happen regularly, or which are always or generally true. We learnt in Lesson 7 that the Present Continuous tense is used to describe actions which are taking place *now* and which continue while the words are said.

In this lesson, we will use the two Tenses together. This will help us to understand the difference in meaning.

Look at the pictures, and read these sentences:

This fat boy *drinks* a lot of milk every day.
He *is not drinking* milk now.
He *is eating* an apple.

This cat *catches* one or two mice every night.
It *is not catching* mice now.
It *is climbing* a tree.

This little girl *runs* to school every morning.
She *is not running* to school now.
She *is putting on* her shoes.

Here is a true sentence, which you can say now, while you are sitting in the classroom and having an English lesson:

I *walk* to school every morning, but I *am not walking* to school now.

Here are similar sentences. Complete them by using a Present Tense or a Present Continuous Tense.

1. I get up at six o'clock, but I — not ———— up now.
2. I wash my hands and face every morning, but I — ——— ———— them now.
3. I clean my teeth every morning, but I — ——— ———— them now.
4. I ——— on my clothes in the morning, but I — ——— putting them on now.
5. I drink water every day, but I — ——— ———— water now.
6. I ——— bread every day, but I — ——— eating bread now.
7. I learn history at school but I — ——— ———— history now.

1. I ——— in the playground, but I — ——— playing now.
2. I go home after school, but I — ——— ———— home now.
3. I help my mother at home, but I — ——— ———— her now.
4. I ———— to the radio every day, but I — ——— listening to it now.
5. I do my homework in the evening, but I — ——— ———— my homework now.
6. I ———— off my clothes at night, but I — ——— taking them off now.
7. I sleep at night, but I — ——— ———— now.

25. The Future Tense

This is the Future Tense of the verb *drink*:

	NEGATIVE	QUESTION
SINGULAR	SINGULAR	SINGULAR
I shall drink.	I shall not drink.	Shall I drink?
You will drink.	You will not drink.	Will you drink?
He will drink.	He will not drink.	Will he drink?
She will drink.	She will not drink.	Will she drink?
It will drink.	It will not drink.	Will it drink?
PLURAL	PLURAL	PLURAL
We shall drink.	We shall not drink.	Shall we drink?
You will drink.	You will not drink.	Will you drink?
They will drink.	They will not drink.	Will they drink?

The Future Tense is made in this way:

shall or *will* + the verb stem *drink*
Negative: *shall* or *will* + *not* + the verb stem *drink*
Question: *shall* or *will* + Subject (Noun or Pronoun) + the verb stem *drink*

We use *shall* with *I* or *we*, and *will* with the other Pronouns.

Practise saying (fairly quickly) the Future Tense, with the Negative and Question forms, of these or of some of these verb stems. First note the irregular verb stem *be*. The Present Tense of *be* is *am, is, are*. Note also the verb stem *have*. We learnt the Present Tense of this verb stem in Lesson 13.

be, have, go, come, walk, run, climb, carry, see, eat.

Put *shall* or *will* in the spaces:

1. Jack _____ be twenty years old in 1980.
2. I _____ get up early tomorrow.
3. The mother _____ take her baby to the doctor tomorrow.
4. We _____ have a holiday next week.
5. My father _____ give me a watch next year.
6. Mary and her sister _____ wear their new dresses tomorrow.
7. I _____ do my homework this evening.
8. We _____ go home after school today.
9. The servant _____ clean the windows tomorrow.
10. I _____ see my mother this evening.

Put *shall* or *will* in the spaces, and make the sentences Negative:

1. The children _____ go to bed late tonight.
2. I _____ come to school tomorrow on my bicycle.
3. Jack's father _____ buy a car this year.
4. Nadia _____ stay at home tomorrow.
5. I _____ see my friend this afternoon.
6. The soldiers _____ sleep in tents tonight.
7. The pupils _____ have new exercise-books next week.
8. The doctor _____ be very busy tomorrow.
9. I _____ play football after school today.
10. The shopkeeper _____ open his shop early tomorrow.

Make questions from these mixed words. Do not forget the capital letter or the question mark.

1. her mother / help / this evening / will she
2. we have / tomorrow / an English lesson / shall
3. early or late / get up / you / will / tomorrow morning.
4. shall / on the blackboard / write / I / the questions
5. all the teachers / be / tomorrow / will / at school
6. on paper / our homework / shall / or in our exercise-books / we do

58

Complete these questions and answers with Future Tenses:

1. How old _____ Jack be in 1980?
   He _____ __ twenty years old.
2. How old _____ Jack's sister be in 1980?
   She _____ __ eighteen years old.
3. Where _____ you be at twelve o'clock tonight?
   I _____ __ in bed.
4. Where _____ the children __ in the summer holiday?
   They _____ go to the seaside.
5. When _____ you see your father?
   I _____ _____ him this evening.
6. When _____ we have our next English lesson?
   We _____ _____ it tomorrow morning.
7. What _____ the boys do after school today?
   They _____ play football.
8. What _____ you __ with your pocket-money next month?
   I _____ buy a penknife.

26. Superlative Adjectives

Look at the pictures of these three boys, and read the sentences:

Jack   Tom   Bob

Jack is a *tall* boy.
He is *taller than* Tom.
He is *taller than* Tom and Bob.
He is *the tallest* boy of the three.
or He is *the tallest* of the three boys.

Bob is a *short* boy.
He is *shorter than* Tom.
He is *shorter than* Tom and Jack.
He is *the shortest* boy of the three.
or He is *the shortest* of the three boys.

We learnt in Lesson 23 that *taller* and *shorter* are the Comparative forms of the Adjectives *tall* and *short*. *tallest* and *shortest* are the Superlative forms, which are made by adding *est* to the Adjectives.

Notice that in these sentences we put *the* before Superlative Adjectives: the tallest, the shortest.

Here are the other Adjectives we used in Lesson 23 with their Comparative and Superlative forms:

ADJECTIVE	COMPARATIVE	SUPERLATIVE
old	older	oldest
young	younger	youngest

rich	richer	richest
poor	poorer	poorest
clean	cleaner	cleanest
cold	colder	coldest
small	smaller	smallest

Notice the spelling in the following Comparative and Superlative forms:

big	bigger	biggest
fat	fatter	fattest
hot	hotter	hottest
thin	thinner	thinnest
dirty	dirtier	dirtiest
happy	happier	happiest
hungry	hungrier	hungriest
pretty	prettier	prettiest

Notice that the following 2 Adjectives have different words in the three forms:

| good | better | best |
| bad | worse | worst |

Read these sentences:

Jack is twelve years old. Tom is ten years old.
Bob is eight years old.

Now complete these sentences:

1. Jack is _____ than Tom.
2. Jack is _____ _____ Tom and Bob.
3. Jack is the _____ boy of the three.
or 4. Jack is ____ _____ of the three boys.
5. Bob is younger _____ Tom.
6. Bob is _____ _____ Tom and Jack.
7. Bob is ____ _____ boy of the three.
or 8. Bob is ____ _____ of the three boys.

Read these sentences:

Jack's father is very rich. Tom's father is not very rich.
Bob's father is very poor.

Now complete these sentences:

1. Jack's father is _____ _____ Tom's father.
2. Jack's father is _____ _____ Tom's father and
   Bob's father.
3. Jack's father is ____ _____ man of the three.
or 4. Jack's father is ____ _____ of the three men.
5. Bob's father is _____ _____ Tom's father.
6. Bob's father is _____ _____ Tom's father and
   Jack's father.
7. Bob's father is ____ _____ man of the three.
or 8. Bob's father is ____ _____ of the three men.

Ask and answer questions like this:

Who is the tallest pupil in this class?
X is the tallest pupil in this class.

Use the Superlative forms of these Adjectives: short, fat, thin, old,
young.

Complete these sentences, using the Superlative forms of the
Adjectives in brackets. Do not forget to put *the* in front of them.

1. The elephant is (big) animal in the world.
2. July and August are (hot) months of the year.
3. December and January are (cold) months of the year.
4. Mary is (pretty) girl in the room.
5. Jack has a new bicycle, and he is (happy) boy in the
   world.
6. My country is (good) in the world.
7. Jack's mark for writing is 8 out of 10. Tom's mark is 6,
   and Bob's mark is 3. Bob has (bad) mark.
8. Jack's face is cleaner than Tom's face. Tom's face is
   cleaner than Bob's face. Bob has (dirty) face.

27. The Possessive Form with *of*

We learnt in Lesson 20 that Possessive forms are made by adding *'s* (apostrophe *s*) or *s'* (*s* apostrophe) to the Noun, for example:

When the possessor is a Singular Noun:

Jack's bicycle, the cat's tail, the child's mother.

When the possessor is a Plural Noun:

The teachers' room, donkeys' ears, the children's mother.

We learnt that these Possessive forms are used with Nouns which are the names of persons, and sometimes with Nouns which are the names of animals. Now look at these two sentences:

The *teacher's keys* are on the table.
The *keys of the cupboard* are on the table, too.

The teacher is a person. He has or possesses keys. The cupboard also has keys, but the cupboard is a thing without life. A cupboard cannot have, or possess, or own keys in the same way as a living person can. So we say *the keys of the cupboard* (NOT *the cupboard's keys*).

The rule is: Use *of* in this way with lifeless things. Here are some examples:

The lid *of* the box
The door *of* the bedroom
The roof *of* the house
The name *of* the street

Use *of* in this way with the words in brackets in the following sentences.

Example: London is (capital-England).
Answer: London is the capital of England.

Example: Do you know (name-street)?
Answer: Do you know the name of the street?

1. The cat is climbing to (top-tree).
2. The servant will wash (floor-classroom) tomorrow.
3. The pupils go out of the classroom at (end-lesson).
4. The policeman is standing in (middle-road).
5. (days-week) are Sunday, Monday, Tuesday, Wednesday, Thursday, Friday, and Saturday.
6. (hands-clock) are pointing at twelve.

28. *can, cannot*

can and *cannot* are used with verb stems like this:

SINGULAR	PLURAL

I can walk,
    but I cannot fly.
	We can walk,
	    but we cannot fly.

You can walk,
    but you cannot fly.
	You can walk,
	    but you cannot fly.

He can walk, but he cannot fly.	

She can walk,
    but she cannot fly.
	They can walk,
	    but they cannot fly.

It can walk, but it cannot fly.	

Notice that *cannot* is ONE word.

can or *cannot* means able or unable to, bodily or mentally. A man can walk (bodily ability), and he can think (mental ability). A baby cannot drive a car (bodily inability), and it cannot read (mental inability).

Put *can* or *cannot* in the spaces:

1. A little child ____ carry a big table.
2. Birds ____ fly, but donkeys ____ fly.
3. My teacher ____ speak English well.
4. I ____ touch the floor, but I ____ touch the ceiling.
5. We ____ wash without soap and water.
6. A rich woman ____ buy a lot of dresses.
7. Cats ____ climb trees, but horses ____ climb trees.
8. We ____ speak a little English.

1. A poor man ____ buy a car.
2. I ____ write with a pencil or with a pen.
3. Little children ____ drive buses.
4. Jack is ill and ____ come to school today.
5. A strong man ____ carry a big box.
6. My mother ____ cook well.
7. I ____ work all day and all night.
8. We ____ go from London to New York by aeroplane.

Questions with *can* are made in this way:

can + Subject (Noun or Pronoun) + verb stem
Example: Can you ride a horse?

or Question word + can + verb stem
Example: Who can answer my question?

or Question word + can + Subject + verb stem
Example: When can you come to the cinema?

Make questions from these mixed words. Do not forget the capital letter or the question mark.

1. the blackboard / can / see / all the pupils
2. and write / a baby / read / can
3. a poor man / a lot of money / can / give his son
4. can / on your head / stand / you
5. pupils / can / learn English / where
6. read / who / the words / can / on the blackboard
7. you see / elephants / can / where / and lions
8. teachers / can / when / have a holiday

66

29. The Adverb

Look at these three sentences:

1. The old man is walking up the hill.
2. The old man is walking *slowly* up the hill.
3. The old man is walking *very slowly* up the hill.

slowly is an Adverb. It adds to the meaning of the verb *is walking*. It answers the question: How is the old man walking?

very is also an Adverb. It adds to the meaning of the Adverb *slowly*. It answers the question: How slowly is the old man walking?

Many Adverbs are made by adding *ly* to Adjectives, for example:

ADJECTIVE	ADVERB
slow	slowly
quick	quickly
bad	badly

Notice the spelling of these 2 Adverbs:

easy	easily
happy	happily

This Adjective and Adverb are the same word:

hard	hard

This Adjective and Adverb are different words:

good	well

Put the above 7 Adverbs into the spaces. Use all 7 Adverbs, each one once only.

1. Lazy men do not work _____
2. The little girl is happy, and is singing _____
3. Rabbits run very _____
4. A tortoise moves very _____
5. The questions are easy, and the pupils can answer them

    _____ .
6. Good pupils read and write _____
7. Bad pupils read and write _____

Now look at this sentence:

Jack goes to bed *early*.

early is an Adverb. It adds to the meaning of the verb *goes* (to bed).
It answers the question: When does Jack go to bed?

Here are 3 more Adverbs which answer questions beginning with
When: late, now, tomorrow.

Put one of these 3 Adverbs into each space:

1. We are sitting in the classroom ____ .
2. We shall come to school ____ .
3. A lazy man gets up ____ in the morning.

Adverbs also answer questions beginning with *Where*. Read these
questions and answers:

Where do you go after school?
I go *home*.

A pupil asks the teacher:

Where shall I sit?

The teacher points to a desk and answers:

Sit *there*.

A pupil asks the teacher:

Where shall I put the chalk?

The teacher points to his table and answers:

Put it *here*.

In these sentences *home*, *there*, and *here* are Adverbs. They add to
the meaning of the verbs *go*, *sit*, and *put*.

30. *must, must not*

must and *must not* are used with verb stems in this way:

1. I *must obey* my father.
2. I *must not play* in class.
3. Pupils *must bring* their books to school every morning.
4. Pupils *must not write* on the walls of the classroom.
5. Little children *must go* to bed early.
6. Little children *must not go* to bed late.

must and *must not* are strong words, which mean *obliged to* or *obliged not to*. If I do not obey my father (Sentence 1), he will punish me. If I play in class (Sentence 2), the teacher will punish me. If little children do not go to bed early (Sentence 5), they will not become strong healthy men and women: there will be a bad result.

Say and/or write the following sentences, putting *must* or *must not* before the verb stems in brackets:

1. You (ride) your bicycle on the pavement.
2. I (clean) my teeth every day.
3. We (come) to school late.
4. We (help) our friends.
5. Pupils (sleep) in the classroom.
6. I (work) hard in school.
7. Pupils (listen) to their teachers.
8. People (be) lazy.
9. A boy (hit) his little brother.
10. We (do) our homework at home.

Questions with *must* are made in the same way as questions with *can* (Lesson 28):

> *must* + Subject (Noun or Pronoun) + verb stem
> *Example:* A little girl asks her mother:
> Must I wear this old dress?

or Question word + *must* + verb stem

Example: Who must work at night?
Answer: Doctors and policemen must work at night.

or Question word + *must* + Subject + verb stem

Example: A little boy asks his mother:
Why must I wash my hands again?

Make questions from the mixed words. Do not forget the capital letters or the question marks.

1. A little boy does not want to go to bed. He asks his father:
   to bed / I / now / go / must
2. The pupils ask the teacher:
   we / on the blackboard / must / all the questions / answer
3. Ahmad has lost a book. His father asks the teacher:
   buy / Ahmad / must / a new book
4. A little girl asks her mother:
   my teeth / must / every day / I / why / clean
5. A teacher of English asks his class:
   must / a full stop / you put / where
6. Jack is ill. His mother asks the doctor:
   how long / in bed / stay / must / Jack

70